Sid and Nan Invent

Written by Nicola Sandford
Illustrated by Jess Mikhail

This is Nan.

She invents things ...
mad things.

She invents things in the shed.

Sid helps Nan invent things.

Nan has a think.

Sid gets the chimp.

Nan gets lots of things ...

They chuck in this.
They fling in that.

They fling in this.
They chuck in that.

Crash!

Bang!

Thud!

13

Has Nan invented an odd-job chimp?

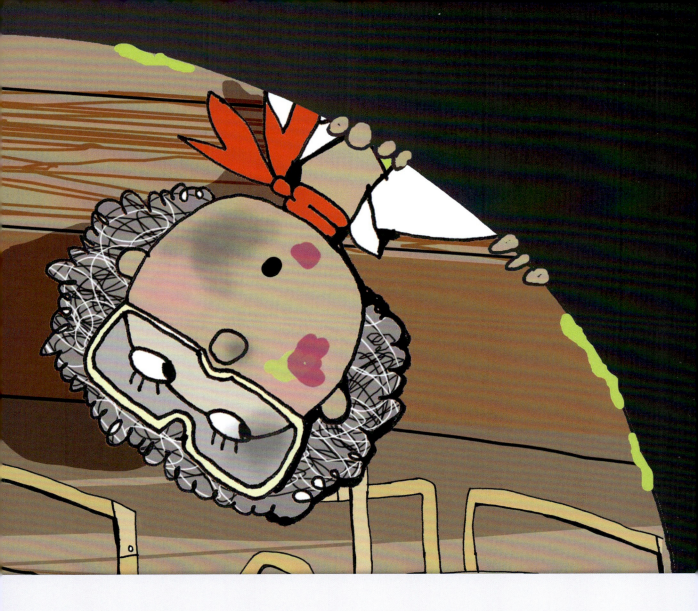

No! Nan has invented an odd chimp ... but she still has the jobs!